The Return of the Woolly Mammoth

T0363429

Written by Joshua Hatch

Illustrated by Kim Woolley

Flying Start
to Literacy®

Contents

Chapter 1

Ancient hunters

Siberia, 40,000 BCE

During the height of the arctic summer, the sun never dips
below the horizon. Instead, it circles overhead, like a halo on
the earth. About 40,000 years ago, a group of hunters used
the never-ending days to search for a herd of mammoths.
Just one mammoth would feed them and their families for a
month. Or, if they were already well fed, they could preserve
the mammoth meat as jerky to eat later during the brutal
arctic winter. Either way, the mammoth was an important
source of food for these nomads.

In the distance, the hunters spotted a herd of mammoths. The mammoths grazed on wispy tufts that grew from the tundra.

As the hunters jogged towards them, they split into groups and tried to hide behind small hills. Approaching the herd, the humans saw six mammoths – four adults and two babies. Hunting mammoths wasn't easy.

The giant pachyderms had long, sharp tusks that could easily kill people; getting close to a mammoth could be deadly. And if you could avoid being impaled, you still had to strike a fatal blow. For that, the hunters relied on long, sharp spears.

The hunters made hand signals to each other. One group would run to the west. The other would circle around to the east. The mammoths had moved into a riverbed and were blocked by the top of a waterfall. So, if the hunters could trap the mammoths, they'd have a good chance of killing one.

The mammoths didn't notice the human hunters until it was too late. As the hunters ran in from each side, the mammoths instinctively gathered together. Then they made the mistake of running towards the waterfall. As soon as they realised they were trapped, the mammoths panicked.

The six mammoths were clumped together, but in their panic, they started to break apart. A large adult male pushed through and dashed past the hunters. The other mammoths tried to follow.

When a small female was slow to make her move, the hunters launched their spears at her. They struck the mammoth. She fell and the humans converged on her, plunging more spears into her. One struck her heart and the mammoth stopped breathing. She would feed the hunters well.

What the hunters didn't notice was that during the commotion, one of the baby mammoths had fallen into the river. Before he could right himself and escape the river's strong current, he was carried over the falls. He wouldn't be seen again for 40,000 years.

Chapter 2

A mammoth find

Siberia, January 2010

Like all winter nights in northern Siberia, this evening was dark and cold. At least, it was outside. Inside our tent, we were warm. A potbelly stove radiated heat from its burning wood, keeping us warm. Reindeer pelts lined the ground and walls.

"I found this today," I said to my wife, Jelena, and her mother, Neda. I pulled out a long white bone. Neda had lived with us ever since her husband died three years before. We liked having her with us. Not only did she help us with our two boys, she also sewed my hunting furs and made the world's best dumplings.

"What is it?" Jelena asked. She was dropping her mother's homemade dumplings into a vat of cooking oil.

"Some kind of bone," I said. "Maybe whale? It's too big to be reindeer. It was sticking out from the ground when I was checking on the herd." Every day, I rode a snowmobile around the tundra to count the reindeer in our herd and drive them towards good grazing land.

"The herd was down by the river," I explained. "And there it was, just glimmering on the river's edge."

"Why would there be a whale bone out by the river?" asked Jelena.

"Not whale," Neda said, barely looking up at the bone. "Mammoth."

"Mammoth?" I asked incredulously.

"Woolly mammoth," she answered. "This is their home. Or it was. They allowed our ancestors to live here, too. Our people survived on their meat. Built tools with their bones. Warmed themselves with their furs."

"But they haven't been here for thousands of years," Jelena said. "Why would their bones appear now?"

"They have always been here," her mother responded. "You just haven't seen them."

Neda's words stuck with me, so the next day I returned to the riverbed to search for more bones. I scanned the banks and saw nothing more than the usual stones and driftwood. As I turned to leave the area and return to the herd, I spotted something unusual in the ledge of a cliff rising up from the river's bank. A light brown object was embedded in the ledge and stretched almost four metres long. It didn't look like the earth around it – it looked like a hairy elephant.

Chapter 3

A dream come true

Brisbane, February 2010

In a university lab in Brisbane, a small woman walked in and announced to her research students: "This is it! This is what we've been waiting for!"

Prisha's students turned to her. None of them had heard the news. They didn't know what Prisha was talking about. They stared at her blankly. She sensed this and added: "An intact woolly mammoth has been found. Perfectly preserved." She paused. "We finally have one!" she shouted excitedly.

Prisha's lab was dedicated to the genetic sequencing of extinct animals. When she was a little girl, she read about woolly mammoths and wished she could have seen them. She even had little toy mammoths, the way other kids had toy horses. Unfortunately, Prisha was thousands of years too late to see them with her own eyes. The species had gone extinct at the end of Earth's last ice age.

Now her wish was about to come true.

"A Siberian reindeer herder found a fully intact mammoth," Prisha started to explain. "It's perfectly preserved. Hair. Tissue. Organs. As fresh as the day it died!"

"What's going to happen to it?" a student named Eve asked.

"It's being taken to the Mammoth Museum in Siberia for further study. They asked me to come and help them with an experiment."

"No way!" Eve said excitedly. "Does that mean what I think it means?"

"Yes," Prisha answered. "This could be the first step towards bringing mammoths back from extinction."

Prisha had always been interested in mammoths, thanks to her mentor, Greg Templeton. He believed some species could be brought back from extinction, if only there was enough good DNA and living species that were genetically similar. Woolly mammoths were first on his list because Asian elephants are closely related to them.

Templeton worked out the science but never had a chance to test it before he died. Still, the idea was straightforward: Take woolly mammoth DNA and inject it into an Asian elephant's egg. Implant the egg into a surrogate elephant and wait.

If all goes well, the embryo will gestate for two years, and the surrogate elephant will give birth to the first woolly mammoth the earth has seen since the last ice age. The process is known as cloning, and it had worked before but never with an extinct species.

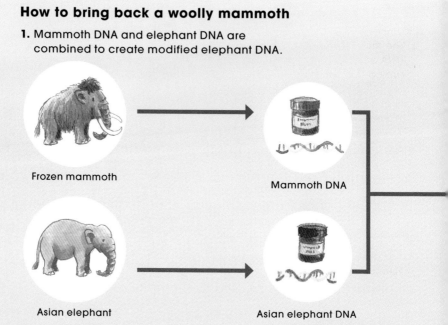

How to bring back a woolly mammoth

1. Mammoth DNA and elephant DNA are combined to create modified elephant DNA.

Frozen mammoth

Mammoth DNA

Asian elephant

Asian elephant DNA

Of course, nobody knows what will happen if it actually works. Will the mammoth be able to drink the surrogate elephant's milk? Where will the mammoth live? Will scientists be able to make more mammoths? Can the entire species come back from extinction and thrive? Templeton never answered these questions. He never even got the mammoth DNA. He just explained how it could be done.

Prisha didn't know the answers to these questions either, but she knew she couldn't miss this chance to test the science. Finally, her dream might come true – to see a real-life woolly mammoth.

2. The modified DNA and egg are combined.

3. The egg is implanted into a surrogate female elephant.

4. A mammoth-elephant hybrid is born two years later.

Modified elephant DNA

Chapter 4

The scientists arrive

Siberia, March 2010

After I spotted the frozen mammoth, I reported it to my
council leaders. They told the experts at the local research
station, who told some scientists about the find. They wanted
to extract the frozen mammoth to study it. We agreed, as long
as they didn't disrupt our herds or damage the areas where
they grazed.

Two months later, a team of scientists showed up on the
riverbank. They had a crane, a flatbed truck and a lot of saws.
The scientists took turns cutting into the frozen earth. They
were careful not to cut too close to the mammoth. The goal
was to carve out a giant block that contained the mammoth,
and then use the crane to lift the block and place it on the
flatbed truck.

It took two weeks for the scientists to cut the mammoth block free, but once they did, the rest of the plan fell into place. The mammoth appeared to be a baby, not a full-grown adult. Still, the block weighed ten tonnes. The crane successfully pulled it from the ledge in the river's bank and set it on the truck. The truck carried it to the Mammoth Museum, and the scientists cleaned up the damage their work had caused to the riverbank.

After they left, I inspected the riverbank to ensure the scientists had caused no damage. Other than the missing section from the ledge, there was no sign the scientists had ever been there. Their camp had been removed. Truck tracks had been cleared away. They did a good job of leaving the area looking like it hadn't been touched.

After checking on the reindeer herd, I returned to my tent. Jelena had made soup and I was eager to eat after a long day on the tundra. The conversation with Jelena and Neda quickly turned to the mammoth.

"Where did they take it?" Jelena asked.

"Back to a museum," I answered.

"They should have left it where it was," Neda spoke up. "It was at peace in the tundra and now it's been disturbed."

"The scientists want to study it," I said.

"The scientists should let the dead rest in peace," Neda said. "If they have questions about the mammoths, ask us." She paused. "The dead have nothing to say."

Chapter 5

The final sequence

Siberia, May 2010

Prisha and Eve caught the first flight they could to Siberia. Once they arrived, they immediately drove to the Mammoth Museum. Their Siberian colleagues had already transported the mammoth from the riverbank to the museum and were in the process of testing samples. To their amazement, the mammoth's hair and skin were perfectly preserved. Tissue samples should provide excellent DNA.

Good DNA was Prisha's goal. She wanted tissue samples that would provide high-quality DNA she could sequence. Sequencing DNA is like decoding a secret message. If you can figure out the pattern, you can read the message. Or, in the case of DNA, you can read the blueprint for making a mammoth!

This was what Prisha had travelled so far for, and her chance to make Templeton's dream come true. They were going to take a tissue sample and try to bring a mammoth back from extinction.

"Are you ready?" one of the Siberian scientists asked. "The DNA in this specimen is exquisitely preserved."

"I'm ready," Prisha said. "I might be crazy, but I'm ready."

"Are you sure you know what you are doing? Have you thought about what it means to bring a woolly mammoth back from extinction?" another scientist asked.

"If this works," Prisha said, "we could reverse decades or hundreds of years of damage we've caused to the ecosystem."

"And if it doesn't?" the scientist persisted.

Prisha thought for a minute. "Then that's no different than our situation today. But we should at least try."

The Siberian scientist relented and he gave Prisha a tissue sample. Elated, she and Eve and the Siberian scientists got to work analysing the sample. For months, they ran experiments and worked to extract usable DNA from the tissue sample. It was painstaking work, but as the seasons changed, Prisha and Eve felt confident they had done it.

"We think this is it," Prisha announced, pointing to a screen. The scientists gathered around. "This appears to be the full sequence." Prisha looked at the screen and the readout of DNA letters – A, T, C and G.

"Is it time to take the next step?" Eve asked. "Time to see if we can inject the DNA into an elephant egg?"

Eve and Prisha looked at each other. They nodded to each other and the Siberian researchers. Smiles crept across their faces.

Chapter 6

Let sleeping mammoths lie

Siberia, September 2020

It's been ten years since I discovered the mammoth in that riverbank. Once or twice a year, the scientists would visit my tent and ask me if I had spotted any new bones or anything else notable. I always kept my eyes open, but I hadn't found anything worth telling the scientists about – only reindeer bones from animals that had gotten too old or succumbed to the cold.

But, during long rides tending the herd, I would wonder what had happened to the little mammoth they carved from the riverbank. When I asked the scientists about it, they would say they were just studying its genetics and how it lived and died. They rarely said much more.

But on the scientists' most recent visit, after we had discussed bone sightings, one of them asked a question that seemed too silly to be taken seriously.

"What about footprints? Or dung?" the scientist asked. "Seen anything like that recently?"

"Footprints? Dung?" I responded, unsure if I had heard correctly.

"That's right," one scientist answered. If she was pulling my leg, she didn't let on.

"No," I answered. "You'd need to go back thousands of years to see anything like that." The scientist looked at me with a smirk. Maybe she was playing a trick on me after all, I thought.

Then, one day a few weeks later – as I pushed my herd towards open land where there was some open grassland not yet buried by snow – I thought I spotted a giant beast on the horizon. It looked like an elephant had been transported to my frozen landscape and covered with a mohair sweater. Its hair shimmered in the wind.

I rubbed my eyes in disbelief and looked again. Whatever it was, it had disappeared. Whether it would ever return, I did not know.

That night in the tent, I told Jelena and Neda what I had seen.

"I swear to you, it was three metres tall and had a coat thicker than ten reindeer pelts," I explained.

"You saw it up close?" Jelena asked.

"No," I admitted. "It was off in the distance. But I know what I saw!" Truthfully, I wasn't entirely sure I had seen it at all. Maybe I had imagined it.

One day when I was in town to buy supplies, I ran into one of the scientists. We talked and she admitted that, yes, they really had returned the woolly mammoth to our world. She tried to explain it to me, but I didn't understand. Something about elephants and eggs.

"Should I be worried?" I asked. "This animal has been gone for thousands of years. It's a different world now."

"That's what we want to see," she replied, her eyes shining brightly.

Of course, I'm the one who has to live with them. It didn't take long to see what the impact of the mammoths would be. Within a few weeks, I noticed one of the grasslands I used for reindeer grazing was trampled. Piles of mammoth dung were scattered where grass once grew. What would my reindeer eat? Later, I found a stream muddied from the mammoths that had trudged through it. What would my reindeer drink? I was worried.

But, as the seasons changed, I realised these changes might not be so bad. The mammoth dung held seeds and helped the grasses spread. And as the mammoths rooted around in the stream, they helped uncover underground springs, which provided more water.

One night, as we sat down to eat, I asked Neda what she thought about the return of the mammoth.

"Like I said," she answered, "they have always been here. Only now are you seeing them."

A note from the author

When I first heard about the idea of bringing woolly mammoths back from extinction, I thought: How wonderful! Humans have caused so many species to go extinct, it would be pretty great if we could undo the damage we've caused.

Then I started to read why de-extinction might not be such a good idea after all. It's expensive and risky, and wouldn't that money be better spent keeping other species from going extinct in the first place? And do we even have a good ecosystem for mammoths to return to?

That got me thinking about what it might look like if mammoths returned. Who would be affected and how? I hope this story got you thinking about this issue, too.